America's
ANIMAL
COMEBACKS

# American Alligators

## Freshwater Survivors

by Aaron Feigenbaum

Consultant: Laura A. Brandt, Ph.D.
U.S. Fish and Wildlife Service
Team Leader, Joint Ecosystem Modeling Lab
Fort Lauderdale Research and Education Center

BEARPORT
PUBLISHING

New York, New York

11/09 30.88

**Credits**

Cover and Title Page, © David Hosking/Alamy; 4, © Thomas McCarver; 5, © William Munoz; 6, © Lynn M. Stone/naturepl.com; 7, © W. Perry Conway/Corbis; 8, © Robert Pickett/Papilio/Alamy; 9, © Martin Woike/FOTO NATURA/Minden Pictures; 10, © Adam White/naturepl.com; 11, © P. Henry/ArcoImages/Peter Arnold, Inc.; 12L, © Lawrence Manning/Corbis; 12R, © W. Perry Conway/Corbis; 13, © The Granger Collection, New York; 14, © Peter Horree/Alamy; 15, © Kevin Fleming/Corbis; 16, © Raymond Gehman/Corbis; 18, © P. Henry/ArcoImages/Peter Arnold, Inc.; 19, © Thomas McCarver; 20, © Thomas McCarver; 21, © Philip Gould/Corbis; 22, © William Munoz; 23, © AP Images/The Post & Courier, Wade Spees; 24, © William Munoz; 25, © C.C. Lockwood/Animals Animals-Earth Scenes; 26, © AP Images/J. Pat Carter; 27, © Stan Osolinski/OSF/Animals Animals-Earth Scenes; 28, © William Munoz; 29T, © Dr. Myrna Watanabe/Peter Arnold, Inc.; 29B, © W. Perry Conway/Corbis; 31, © magmarcz/Shutterstock.

Publisher: Kenn Goin
Senior Editor: Lisa Wiseman
Creative Director: Spencer Brinker
Photo Researcher: Amy Dunleavy
Cover Design: Dawn Beard Creative

*Library of Congress Cataloging-in-Publication Data*

Feigenbaum, Aaron.
  American alligators : freshwater survivors / by Aaron Feigenbaum.
    p. cm. — (America's animal comebacks)
  Includes bibliographical references and index.
  ISBN-13: 978-1-59716-503-7 (library binding)
  ISBN-10: 1-59716-503-4 (library binding)
  1. American alligator—Juvenile literature. I. Title.

  QL666.C925F45 2008
  597.98′4—dc22

                    2007013160

For more information, write to Bearport Publishing Company, Inc., 101 Fifth Avenue, Suite 6R, New York, New York 10003. Printed in the United States of America.

10 9 8 7 6 5 4 3 2 1

# Contents

# Visiting the Nests

It was a hot, sticky day in July 2000. **Biologist** Walt Rhodes sloshed through the muddy waters of the Santee Coastal **Reserve** in South Carolina. He was looking for alligator nests filled with eggs. When he found a nest, he stuck his hands into it.

"Ouch!" he cried.

Walt Rhodes checks on an alligator nest.

A mother alligator can lay between 20 to 70 eggs. Only about 7 to 10 of the babies will survive. The rest will be eaten by other animals, such as birds and raccoons.

Fire ants stung his arms. Walt ignored the pain. He needed to quickly take the temperature of the nest to find out when the eggs would hatch. Then he would check on some of the other nests.

Soon Walt returned to his boat. The stings hurt, but at least he hadn't run into a mother alligator. She would not have been happy to find him touching her eggs.

Not long ago, Walt would have had few eggs to study. In the mid-1900s, American alligators were on the brink of **extinction**.

An American alligator

5

# Long Ago

American alligators have lived on Earth for more than 200 million years. Very few kinds of living creatures have been on Earth that long. Alligators ruled the swamps before dinosaurs roamed the land!

Alligators have an extra eyelid on each eye. It helps protect their eyes. The eyelid is clear so alligators can see under water.

Millions of alligators once lived in what is today the southeastern United States. The warm weather is good for them because they are **cold-blooded**. Alligators need warm weather to help keep their body temperature up. The **region** also provides the perfect **environment** for them. Alligators live both on land and in water. The Southeast is filled with lakes, rivers, ponds, and **wetlands**.

Alligators cool off by swimming in the water.

# Tall Tales

Thousands of years ago, Native Americans came to live in the Southeast. They began hunting and killing alligators for their body parts. They ate the alligator's meat. Alligator skins were used to make drums. Some tribes wore the gator's teeth and bones around their necks. They thought these alligator parts kept away some illnesses.

Alligators have very strong jaws and more than 70 sharp teeth.

Then in the 1600s, French explorers began to arrive. They hunted these **reptiles** for a different reason—fear. The explorers thought the gators were fierce monsters. One explorer told stories of the animal growing to be "25 feet (8 m) long" and feasting on bulls. Another claimed that the animal's roar "could be heard a half-mile (.8 km)" away. Much of what they said was not true. However, these **tall tales** led people to fear alligators.

Alligators don't usually eat large animals. They like to snack on fish, snakes, turtles, small mammals, and birds.

# A Big Misunderstanding

Were settlers right to fear alligators? The reptiles did sometimes attack **livestock** and people. They still do today. However, the number of attacks is very small. Alligators killed 17 people from 1948 to 2006.

This alligator stays far away from the woman in the kayak.

However, from the 1600s though the 1800s, early settlers knew only that alligators looked scary and mysterious. What they didn't know is that these creatures are shy. Alligators don't want to be close to people. Most of the time they run or swim away from humans. They may attack if they feel **threatened** or to protect their nests.

Without knowing this, many settlers continued to think that alligators were a danger. Many people killed them out of fear.

Mother alligators are very protective of their nests.

Every year, bees and dogs injure and kill more people than alligators do.

# Hunting Season

In 1855, American settlers began hunting and killing alligators for a new reason. Designers in France had discovered that they could use alligator skins to make leather products, such as bags and shoes. These items became very popular. Americans hunted the alligators and sold the skins to the French. Americans were not only getting rid of the animals they feared, they were also making money, too.

A shoe and pocketbook made from alligator skin

Then in 1870, factories in the United States started using alligator skins to make clothes and bags. Before long, hunters were killing thousands of alligators every year. By the mid-1900s, hunters had killed more than 10 million alligators.

An alligator hunt, in 1874, down the St. Johns River in Florida

Between 1881 and 1891, hunters killed more than two million alligators.

# Desperate Measures

Hunting wasn't the only problem these reptiles were facing. They were losing their homes, too. As people moved to the Southeast, they built houses and businesses on the gator's **habitat**. The new construction also caused parts of the wetlands to become **polluted**. The gators had no choice but to find new homes. However, as more people moved into the area, it got harder for them to find places to live.

Wetlands, such as the Everglades in Florida, need to be preserved in order to save the alligator.

Finally in the 1960s, scientists sounded an alarm— alligators were in trouble. Hunting and habitat loss had killed too many of them. Few remained in the wild. In Louisiana alone, the gator **population** declined by more than 90 percent. Something had to be done fast to save these creatures.

A housing development built on wetlands in the Florida Everglades

The largest American alligator ever caught was more than 19 feet (6 m) long. It was found in Louisiana.

# Back from the Brink

Finally state governments started to take action. In 1961, Florida made alligator hunting against the law. Then Louisiana banned it a year later. **Poachers**, however, continued to kill alligators and sell their skins to **traders**. By 1967, there were so few alligators left that they were declared **endangered** in Florida.

This ranger searches for poachers on Lake Kissimmee in Florida.

Three years later, the U.S. government passed a law that made it **illegal** to buy and sell alligators. Officials fined traders and even sent some to jail. Traders stopped buying alligators from poachers. Since nobody was buying skins, poachers stopped making money. They soon stopped hunting alligators altogether.

These new laws allowed alligators to increase their numbers. In 1987, the government changed the listing for alligators. It went from *endangered* to *threatened*. Gators are no longer in danger of becoming extinct. However, alligator skins and products are still being **regulated**.

☐ **Where American alligators live today**

In 1970, only about 170,000 alligators lived in Louisiana. Today, there are more than 2 million.

# Studying Alligators

Government officials realized that people didn't know enough about alligators. If they learned more about these reptiles, then maybe they could help them survive. So the government decided to give scientists money to study alligators.

Scientists sometimes take blood from alligators to learn more about them.

Scientists help set limits on the number of alligators that can be hunted each year.

Walt Rhodes is one of the scientists studying gators. He has been working with these reptiles for more than 15 years. He says that his job is not dangerous. However, he jokes that he has "set the world record for the most fire ant bites."

Walt received a few more bites in July 2000 when he checked the temperature of several nests in the Santee Coastal Reserve. The temperature told him that the eggs would **hatch** in September.

Walt checking on some eggs

# The Eggs

Walt returned to the reserve in mid-August to collect the eggs. He would **incubate** them in his backyard for the final weeks before they hatched. Then he would study the babies.

When the temperature in an alligator nest is above 90°F (32°C), all the babies will be male. If it's less than 86°F (30°C), all the babies will be female. A nest between these temperatures contains both males and females.

At home, Walt watched the temperature of the eggs carefully. He had to make sure they stayed at the same temperature as they were in the nests. Otherwise, the babies inside the eggs might die. If they started getting too hot, he cooled the eggs down with water from a hose. At night, he covered them to make sure they stayed warm.

Alligator eggs are about the same size as goose eggs.

# Backyard Babies

When the eggs hatched, Walt moved the **hatchlings** to special pens that contained wet areas. Just as alligators born in the wild do, the baby alligators started swimming immediately.

Walt checked the babies to see how many males and females were in the group. Only females lay eggs. If there are fewer females, then there will be fewer alligators later on. This can put the gator population in danger. Happily, Walt found that there were plenty of females.

Baby alligators hatching

Walt also measured and weighed each baby. If they were smaller than usual, he would know that something was wrong. Pollution or other environmental problems can affect gators. This year, however, the babies were normal size. The reserve's environment seemed safe for now.

One of Walt's hatchlings takes his first look at the world.

Alligator babies are only 6 to 8 inches (15 to 20 cm) long when they are born. It takes about 6 to 12 years for an alligator to grow to 6 feet (2 m) in length.

# Return to Nature

After studying the baby alligators for a few weeks, Walt returned them to the reserve. He dropped them off in the very same nests where he had picked them up.

Only young alligators have stripes.

Soon, the hatchlings started squealing. Their mothers heard them and returned to their nests. Walt watched from a distance as the hatchlings followed their mothers into the water. Some couldn't make it and had to be carried in their mothers' mouths. Once each family was in the water, they swam away.

Mother alligators will stay with their hatchlings and protect them from **predators** for at least a year.

A mother carrying a baby in her mouth

# The Future

The future of the American alligator looks bright. More than four million alligators live in the Southeast today. Government officials still regulate hunting. Most of the alligator shoes, belts, and bags found in stores today come from gators raised on farms. This reptile continues to be listed as threatened and not endangered.

Feeding time at an alligator farm

However, all is not perfect. People are continuing to move to the Southeast, causing gators to lose their homes. This loss brings alligators and humans into closer contact, which can be dangerous.

In response to these problems, scientists such as Walt Rhodes try to teach people about alligators. They want to make it possible for people and alligators to live together safely.

In 1987, the alligator became the official state reptile of Florida.

# Alligator Facts

In 1973, Congress passed the Endangered **Species** Act. This law protects animals and plants that are in danger of dying out in the United States. Harmful activities, such as hunting, capturing, or collecting endangered species, are illegal under this act.

**The American alligator was one of the first species listed under the Endangered Species Act. Here are some other facts about the American alligator.**

**Population:**    **North American population in 1600:** unknown

                     **North American population today:** more than 4 million

| Weight | Average Length | Color |
|---|---|---|
| up to 1,000 pounds (454 kg) | females: about 8 feet (2.4 m)<br>males: about 13 feet (3.9 m) | black; very rarely white |

| Food | Habitat | Life Span |
|---|---|---|
| fish, snakes, turtles, small mammals, and birds | swamps, marshes, rivers, lakes, ponds, and wetlands from North Carolina to Texas | about 40 years in the wild; about 50 years in captivity |

# Other Alligators in Danger

American alligators are one kind of animal in the alligator family making a comeback by increasing their numbers. Other animals in this family are also trying to make a comeback.

## Chinese Alligator

- Chinese alligators live near the Yangtze River in southern China.

- There are fewer than 200 Chinese alligators living in the wild.

- The biggest problem facing these animals is habitat loss.

- Scientists are breeding Chinese alligators and reintroducing them back into the wild to try to increase their numbers.

## Black Caiman

- Black caimans live in South America.

- There are between 25,000 and 50,000 black caimans in the wild.

- Overhunting reduced the number of black caimans by 99 percent over the past 100 years.

- A hunting ban and many breeding programs are helping black caimans make a comeback.

# Glossary

**biologist** (bye-OL-uh-jist)
a scientist who studies plants or animals

**cold-blooded** (KOHLD-BLUHD-id)
having a body temperature that changes with the temperature of the environment

**endangered** (en-DAYN-jurd)
being in danger of dying out

**environment** (en-VYE-ruhn-muhnt)
the plants, animals, and weather in a place

**extinction** (ek-STINGK-shuhn)
when no members of a kind of plant or animal group are still alive

**habitat** (HAB-uh-*tat*)
a place in nature where plants or animals normally live

**hatch** (HACH)
to come out of an egg

**hatchlings** (HACH-lingz)
young babies that came from an egg

**illegal** (i-LEE-guhl)
against the law

**incubate** (ING-kyuh-bate)
to hatch eggs by keeping them warm

**livestock** (LIVE-*stok*)
animals, such as sheep, chicken, or cows, that are raised on a farm or ranch

**poachers** (POHCH-urz)
people who hunt animals illegally

**polluted** (puh-LOOT-id)
contaminated or made dirty

**population** (*pop*-yuh-LAY-shuhn)
the total number of people or animals living in a place

**predators** (PRED-uh-turz)
animals that hunt other animals for food

**region** (REE-juhn)
an area

**regulated** (REG-yuh-late-id)
controlled by the government

**reptiles** (REP-tilez)
cold-blooded, egg-laying animals that have a backbone

**reserve** (ri-SURV)
a protected place where animals can live safely

**species** (SPEE-sheez)
groups that animals are divided into, according to similar characteristics; members of the same species can have offspring together

**tall tales** (TAWL TAYLZ)
stories that are not true

**threatened** (THRET-uhnd)
being in immediate danger

**traders** (TRAY-derz)
people who exchange goods for other goods

**wetlands** (WET-landz)
land that has water in the soil

# Bibliography

**McClintock, Jack.** "Alligators Live Forever," *Discover*, vol. 22: no. 5 (2001).

**Morrison, Susan Dudley.** *The Alligator.* Mankato, MN: Crestwood House (1984).

**Patent, Dorothy Hinshaw.** *The American Alligator.* New York: Clarion Books (1994).

**Scott, Jack Denton.** *Alligator.* New York: G. P. Putnam's Sons (1984).

# Read More

**Rockwell, Anne.** *Who Lives in an Alligator Hole?* New York: HarperCollins (2006).

**Simon, Seymour.** *Crocodiles & Alligators.* New York: HarperTrophy (1999).

**Staub, Frank.** *Alligators.* Minneapolis, MN: Lerner Publications Company (1995).

# Learn More Online

To learn more about alligators, visit
**www.bearportpublishing.com/AnimalComebacks**

# Index

# About the Author

Aaron Feigenbaum is an anthropologist, editor, and children's book author. He currently resides in New York City.